CLEOPATRA

DIANE STANLEY · PETER VENNEMA

ILLUSTRATED BY DIANE STANLEY

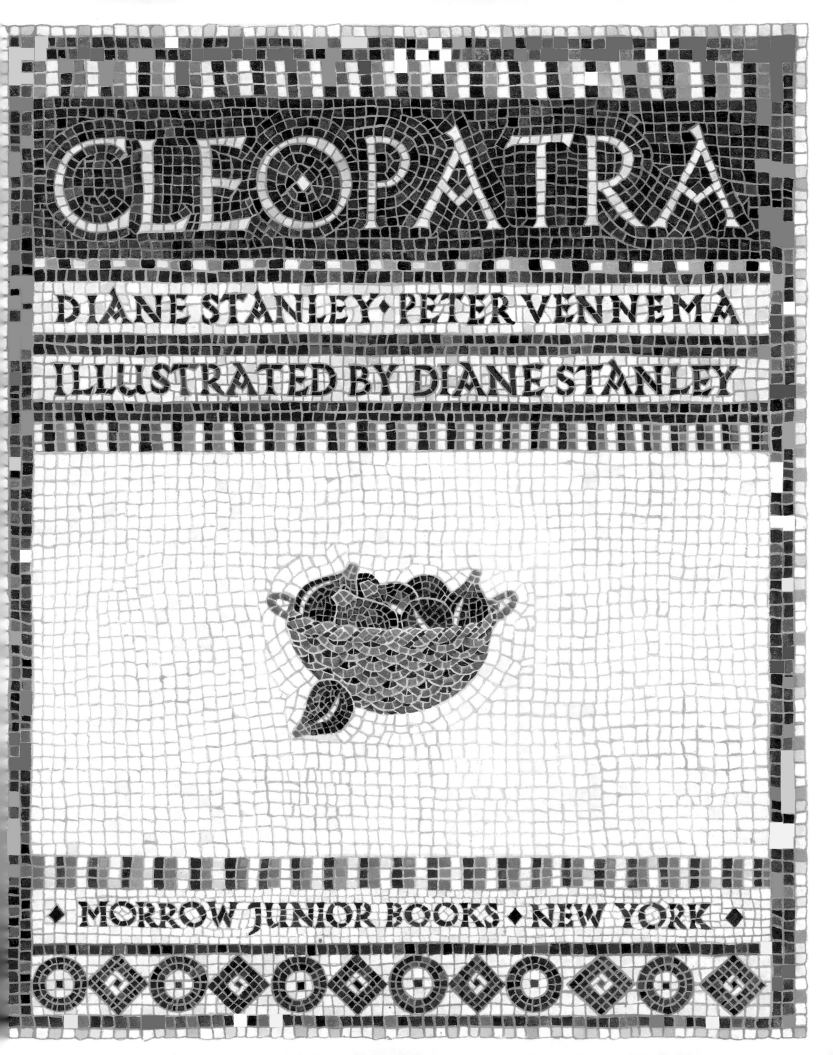

MORROW JUNIOR BOOKS · NEW YORK

For my daughter Tamara,
wordsmith extraordinaire, with love
—D. S.

The authors gratefully acknowledge the careful reading and advice of Dr. Rebecca Mersereau,
Assistant Professor in the Department of Art and Art History, Rice University,
and Dr. Diana Delia, Associate Professor of Ancient History, Texas A&M University.

Gouache was used for the full-color artwork. The text type is 13-point Korinna.

Printed in Hong Kong by South China Printing Company (1988) Ltd.

1 2 3 4 5 6 7 8 9 10

Library of Congress Cataloging-in-Publication Data
Stanley, Diane.
Cleopatra / Diane Stanley and Peter Vennema;
illustrated by Diane Stanley.
p.   cm.
Includes bibliographical references.
ISBN 0-688-10413-4 (trade). — ISBN 0-688-10414-2 (library)
1 Cleopatra, Queen of Egypt, d. 30 B.C.—Juvenile literature.
2. Queens—Egypt—Biography—Juvenile literature. [1. Cleopatra,
Queen of Egypt, d. 30 B.C. 2. Kings, queens, rulers, etc.]
I. Vennema, Peter. II. Title.
DT92.7.S84 1994
932'.021—dc20   93-27032 CIP AC

PREFACE

Many people believe that Cleopatra was one of the ancient queens of Egypt. But, in fact, she did not live in the days of the Pharaohs. When she was born, in 69 B.C., the pyramids had already been standing for more than twenty-five hundred years. She was not even Egyptian. Cleopatra was Macedonian Greek, the last of the Ptolemies, a royal line descended from a general of Alexander the Great.

Alexander had taken Egypt from the Persians in 331 B.C. He founded a new capital there in the Greek style, which he named Alexandria, after himself. When he died only eight years later, his body was returned to Alexandria for burial. His vast empire was divided up among his generals, and Egypt fell to Ptolemy, who made himself King Ptolemy I. Ptolemy wanted to rule in the style of the ancient Pharaohs. So he used their titles and claimed to be a god in human form, as they had. He also revived the custom of brother-sister marriages in the royal family.

In spite of this effort to identify with Egypt, the Ptolemies remained essentially Greek. It is a telling fact that of all the Ptolemies, only Cleopatra ever bothered to learn the Egyptian language.

At that time, Alexandria was said to be the most beautiful city in the world. But it was also a great center for learning. Poets, philosophers, and scientists

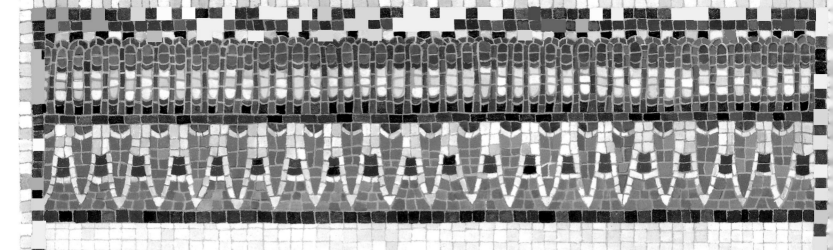

came from far and wide to study at the Museum, the forerunner of our modern universities. It was a physician in Alexandria who discovered the circulation of blood. It was there that Euclid formulated his principles of geometry. And it was an Alexandrian astronomer, brought to Rome by Julius Caesar, who gave the Egyptian calendar to the West. Cleopatra's capital had the world's finest library and its tallest building—the Pharos lighthouse, one of the seven wonders of the ancient world.

But for all of Alexandria's grandeur and Egypt's wealth, the real power in the Western world was Rome. Unlike Egypt, ruled by god-kings, Rome had been a republic for almost five hundred years. This meant the Roman people were governed by an elected senate. Rome was a mighty military force, controlling vast territories in Europe, Asia, and Africa. Egypt, which had once conquered other lands, now lived under Rome's shadow.

At the time our story opens, Julius Caesar had effective control of Rome and all its provinces. He would soon have titles and authority unmatched in the history of the republic. Caesar and his successors, Mark Antony and Octavian, saw military conquest as a noble enterprise and dreamed of a world united under Roman rule. Cleopatra had similar goals, but she envisioned a combined empire ruled from Alexandria by the Ptolemies. And she almost succeeded. At the height of her power, Cleopatra rallied the wealth and might of Asia to her cause and made proud Rome tremble.

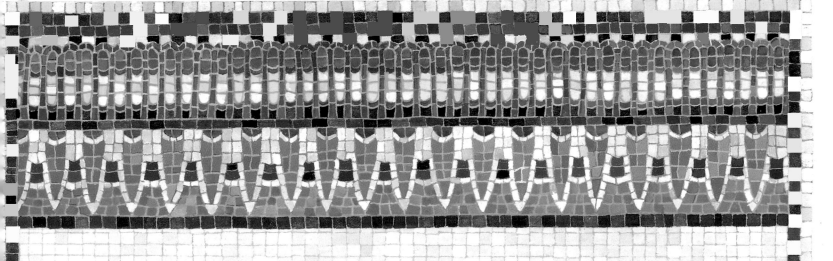

NOTE ON ANCIENT SOURCES

Everything we know about Cleopatra was written by her enemies. It is not surprising, then, that she was portrayed as a conniving, immoral woman. There must have been accounts of her life written by her supporters, but they have not survived. Probably the Romans destroyed them.

We know what Julius Caesar, Mark Antony, and Octavian looked like from the beautifully carved statues made of them. We are not so lucky where Cleopatra is concerned, for her statues were torn down. The most reliable sources for what she looked like are the many coins bearing her profile. The carving on them is crude, but we can tell how she wore her hair and that she had a prominent nose and chin.

Cleopatra's life story comes from many sources, but the dramatic episodes of her later life come mostly from Plutarch, a Greek historian. He wrote a book in which he compared the lives of famous Greeks and Romans. It is in the chapter on Mark Antony that the Queen of Egypt truly comes alive for us. No other account gives us such rich details and vivid anecdotes, and all historians who have written about her since have turned frequently to Plutarch—but with caution. First, he lived a hundred years after Cleopatra, and much of what he writes may have been mere gossip or legend. Second, many of his sources were influenced by the propaganda put forth by the conquering Octavian and his supporters. Even so, Cleopatra shines through the narrative like the exceptional woman she was, and in the end, like Caesar and Antony before him, Plutarch could not resist her.

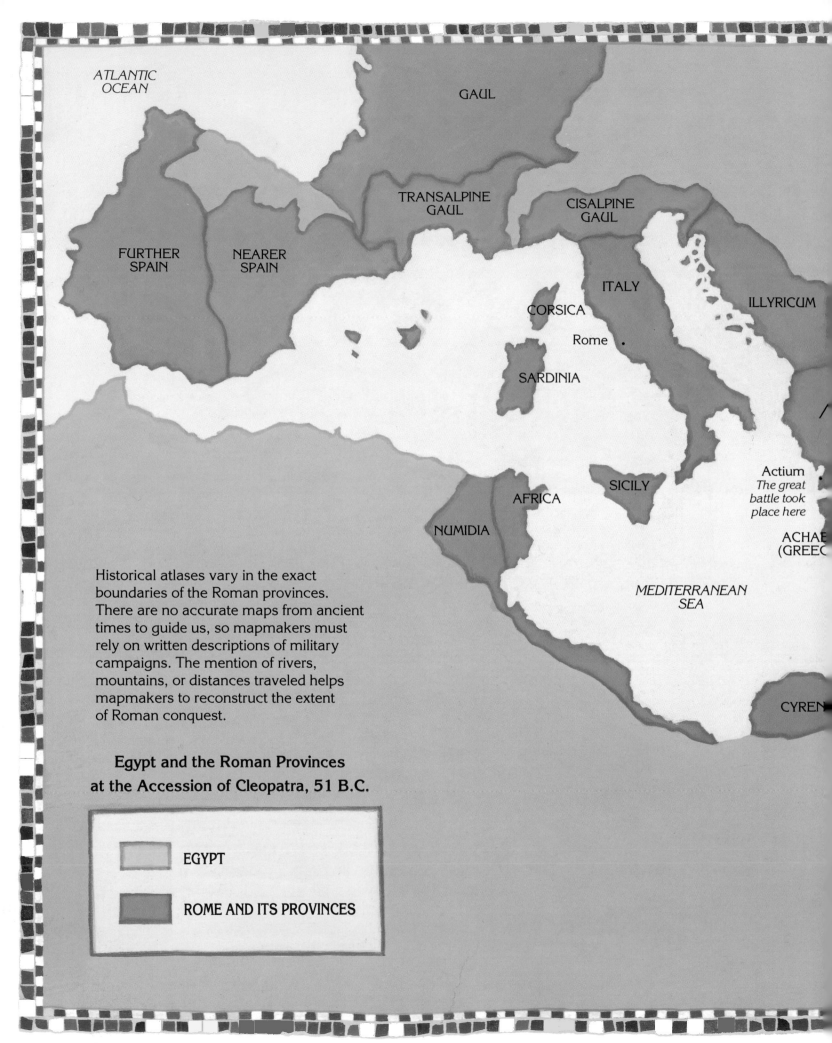

ATLANTIC
OCEAN

GAUL

TRANSALPINE
GAUL

CISALPINE
GAUL

FURTHER
SPAIN

NEARER
SPAIN

ITALY

ILLYRICUM

CORSICA

Rome

SARDINIA

Actium
*The great
battle took
place here*

SICILY

ACHAE
(GREEC

AFRICA

NUMIDIA

Historical atlases vary in the exact
boundaries of the Roman provinces.
There are no accurate maps from ancient
times to guide us, so mapmakers must
rely on written descriptions of military
campaigns. The mention of rivers,
mountains, or distances traveled helps
mapmakers to reconstruct the extent
of Roman conquest.

MEDITERRANEAN
SEA

CYREN

**Egypt and the Roman Provinces
at the Accession of Cleopatra, 51 B.C.**

EGYPT

ROME AND ITS PROVINCES

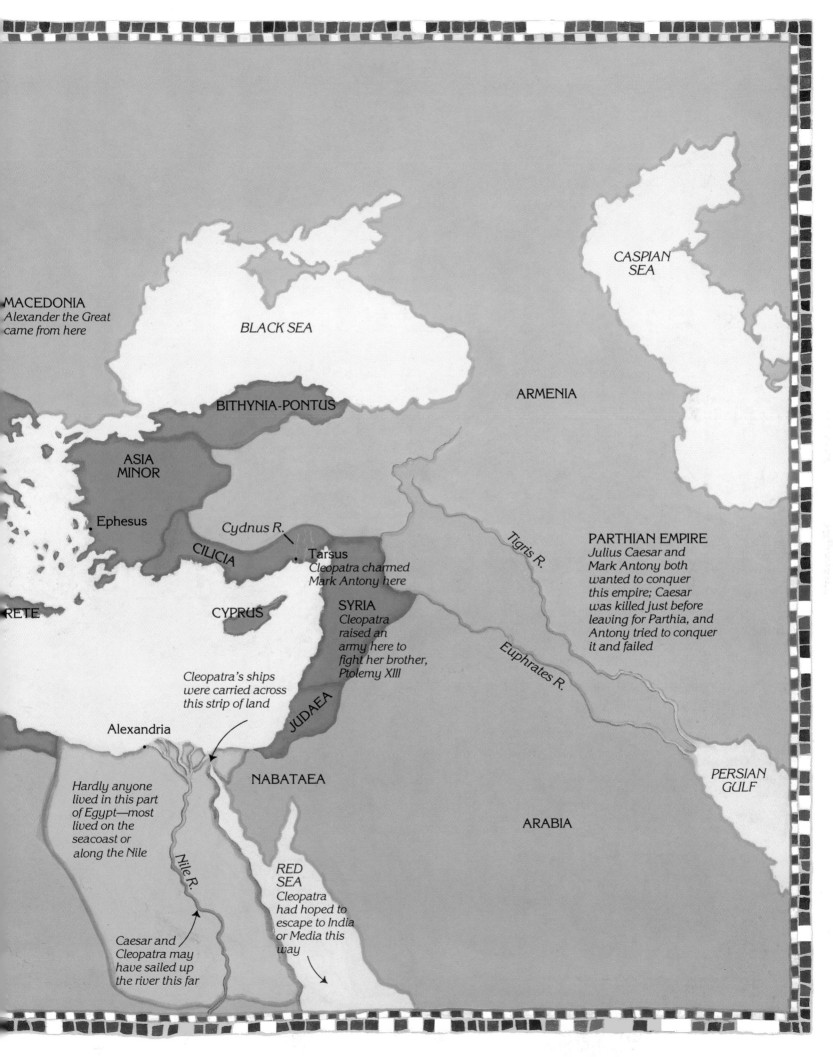

MACEDONIA
*Alexander the Great
came from here*

BLACK SEA

CASPIAN
SEA

ARMENIA

BITHYNIA-PONTUS

ASIA
MINOR

• Ephesus

Cydnus R.

CILICIA

• Tarsus
*Cleopatra charmed
Mark Antony here*

CYPRUS

SYRIA
*Cleopatra
raised an
army here to
fight her brother,
Ptolemy XIII*

Tigris R.

PARTHIAN EMPIRE
*Julius Caesar and
Mark Antony both
wanted to conquer
this empire; Caesar
was killed just before
leaving for Parthia, and
Antony tried to conquer
it and failed*

Euphrates R.

RETE

*Cleopatra's ships
were carried across
this strip of land*

JUDAEA

• Alexandria

NABATAEA

PERSIAN
GULF

*Hardly anyone
lived in this part
of Egypt—most
lived on the
seacoast or
along the Nile*

ARABIA

Nile R.

RED
SEA
*Cleopatra
had hoped to
escape to India
or Media this
way*

*Caesar and
Cleopatra may
have sailed up
the river this far*

Cleopatra VII was eighteen years old when she became Queen of Egypt in the year 51 B.C. As was the custom, she ruled together with her brother, Ptolemy XIII, who was only ten. As was also the custom, Ptolemy became her husband. This was only a formality, though, since he was still a child.

The young king was guided by three important advisers. Since the male was traditionally the chief ruler, these three men expected to rule the country in Ptolemy's name.

But Cleopatra was strong-willed and ambitious. She longed to return her country to the glory of its earlier years. Perhaps Egypt could even regain the empire it had once had under the warlike Pharaoh Thutmose III, fourteen hundred years before. Cleopatra wanted to accomplish this herself, but Ptolemy's advisers were stronger than the young queen. By the time Cleopatra was twenty, they had driven her out of Egypt.

Cleopatra was determined to fight for the throne, so she raised an army in Syria and prepared to go to war against her brother. But before the battle could begin, it was interrupted by the arrival in Alexandria of Julius Caesar, the most powerful man in Rome. He was pursuing his defeated rival in a Roman civil war.

Finding his enemy already dead and Egypt on the verge of a civil war of its own, Caesar moved into the palace and tried to make peace. He sent messages to the two rulers, urging them to abandon the battle and return to Alexandria to settle their differences. Ptolemy came, but his advisers were afraid Cleopatra might win Caesar's support. So they had the palace surrounded by soldiers and ordered them to kill the queen if she tried to get in.

But Cleopatra thought of a plan. She sailed to Alexandria, anchoring the ship offshore. Then she and a man named Apollodorus took a small boat and entered the harbor at nightfall. Once they were safely ashore, Apollodorus wrapped her up in a roll of bedding (some say it was a rug) and carried her into the palace. He delivered the bedroll to Caesar—who must have been amazed and delighted when it was unrolled to reveal the queen.

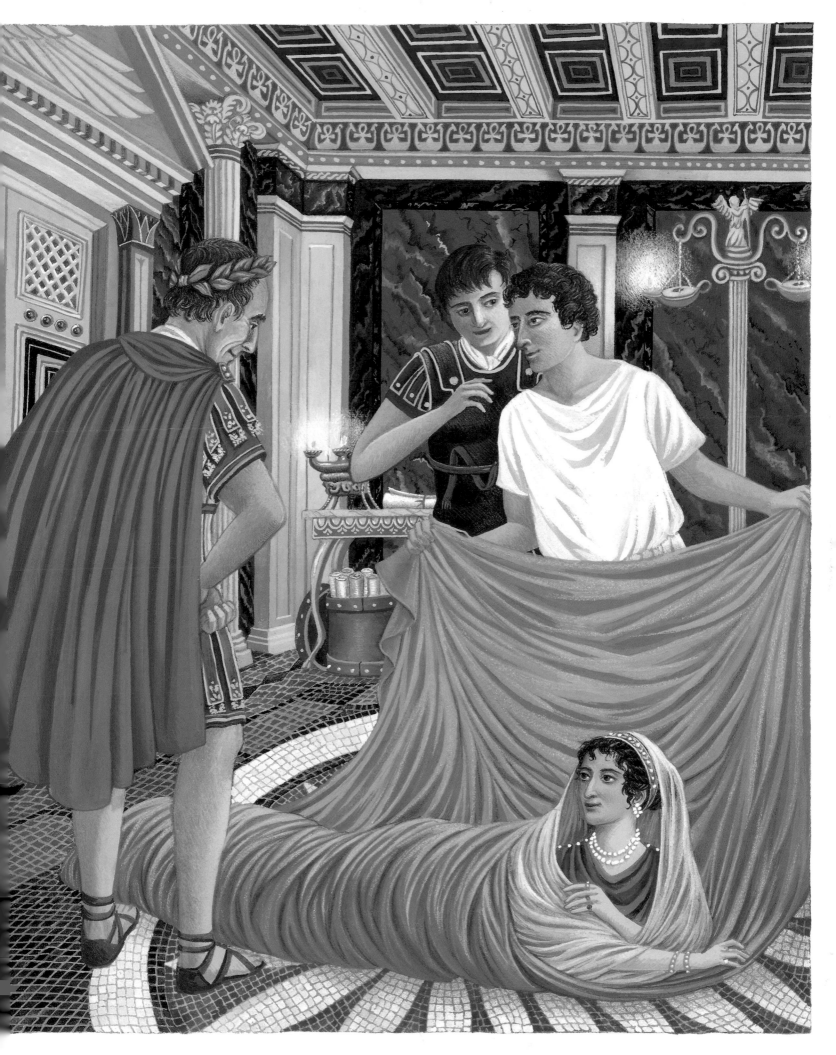

That evening began one of history's great love stories. Julius Caesar, at fifty-two, was at the height of his career. He was a brilliant, brave, and confident general who had conquered much of Europe. He was probably the most famous and powerful man in the world.

Though Cleopatra was only twenty when she met this great man, she was hardly an awestruck girl. In fact, they met as equals, for she too had a brilliant mind and a fine education. She was descended from an ancient royal line and was worshiped as a goddess by her people. And the wealth of the Ptolemies was legendary.

It is traditionally believed that Cleopatra dazzled Caesar with her great beauty. Instead, it was the power of her intelligence and personality that drew him to her. According to Plutarch, "the charm of her presence was irresistible, and there was an attraction in her person and her talk, together with a peculiar force of character which pervaded her every word and action, and laid all who associated with her under its spell."

From that night, these two exceptional people lived as man and wife.

Caesar had hoped to persuade Ptolemy to settle peacefully with Cleopatra, but it came to war in the end. The next six months saw a siege of the palace, the poisoning of its drinking water, the burning of the Egyptian fleet, and battles on sea and land. At last, Ptolemy's army was defeated, and the fifteen-year-old king drowned in the Nile, weighed down by his golden armor. Cleopatra was crowned once again as queen, this time sharing the throne with her youngest brother, also named Ptolemy, who ruled as Ptolemy XIV.

Though Caesar should have hurried back to Rome, he was eager to see more of Egypt. So Cleopatra planned a cruise up the Nile for him. The royal barge was made ready, and for many luxurious weeks they sailed upriver to view the magnificent remains of three thousand years of Egyptian culture.

This rich and fertile land and the grandeur of its ancient civilization must have stirred such an ambitious man. As powerful as he was, his country was

a republic, and he held an elected position. But to be a king, a god—that would be far better. If he were to marry this dazzling queen, between them they would control most of the known world. As her husband, he would become a divine king. Their child—soon to be born—would rule after him.

Cleopatra dreamed the same dream, but in her efforts to attain it, she would sacrifice everything.

Caesar was enjoying himself so much that he stayed and stayed. His worried generals finally persuaded him to get back to business. Reluctantly, he left Egypt to tend to matters in Asia Minor, and soon after, he returned to Rome. Cleopatra joined him there with their baby son, Ptolemy Caesar, whom she called Caesarion. Cleopatra moved into Caesar's country estate, and he often visited her there. This scandalized the people of Rome, for Caesar already had a wife.

Soon Roman tongues were wagging about her mountains of baggage, her many servants, and her lavish ways. But perhaps the most shocking moment came when Julius Caesar had a statue made of Cleopatra and placed it in a temple of Venus, thus declaring her to be a goddess—not only in Egypt but also in Rome!

The city buzzed with rumors that Caesar was planning to make himself king, with Cleopatra as his queen, and that the capital would be moved to Alexandria.

Caesar's behavior certainly supported the rumors. He began to sit on a golden throne in the senate. He even had a statue of himself placed beside those of the seven kings of ancient Rome.

Those who believed in the republic were afraid of Caesar's ambition. And so, in the spring of the year 44 B.C., Brutus and Cassius, two men whom Caesar knew and trusted, formed a conspiracy to assassinate him. They were joined by sixty to eighty other senators. The day they chose was March 15, called the Ides (or middle day) of March.

On the night of March 14, Caesar's wife had a terrible dream in which her husband was killed. The next morning she begged him not to leave the house, for there had been other warnings as well. The most famous was from a soothsayer who had stopped him on the street and whispered, "Beware the Ides of March!" Caesar hesitated. But the conspirators sent a message urging him to come to the senate. To make sure he would, they told him that on that day he would be made king of all the Roman provinces. So Julius Caesar went to the senate. When he arrived, the assassins, many of them his friends, fell upon Caesar and murdered him.

In one stroke, Cleopatra seemed to have lost everything—the man she loved and all her grand hopes. Fearing she might also lose her life, she quickly returned to Egypt.

When Caesar's will was read, it made no mention of his son, Caesarion. Instead, it was Octavian, his eighteen-year-old grandnephew, whom he adopted and made his heir. It soon became clear that Octavian hoped to inherit not only his adoptive father's money and estates but also his position as the most important man in Rome.

For the moment, that position was held by Mark Antony. He was a great general and a statesman who had won the loyalty of the soldiers and the admiration of the Roman people. Antony's position was so strong that he hardly took Octavian seriously. But Octavian proved to be more clever and determined than anyone might have guessed.

At last, Antony and Octavian arrived at a compromise. Together with another prominent Roman named Marcus Aemilius Lepidus, they sought out the assassins and brought them to justice. Then they agreed to govern the Roman territories together, eventually dividing them three ways. Antony took the eastern provinces, Octavian took those in the west, and Lepidus was given Africa. Later, this three-man rule (called a triumvirate) began to break down. Octavian forced Lepidus out and took Africa. The ultimate struggle for supremacy was to be between Antony and Octavian.

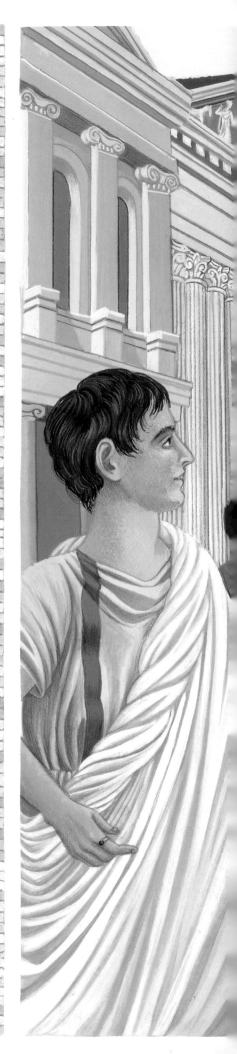

As soon as Brutus and Cassius were defeated, Antony left Rome and headed east on a military campaign. On the way, he stopped at Tarsus, in Cilicia. He then sent a message to Egypt, ordering Cleopatra to meet him there. He had matters he wished to discuss with her. The messenger recommended that she come in "all the splendor her art could command." But the queen chose not to answer the summons. Antony sent another message and yet another. Still Cleopatra refused to respond. Though she planned to come to Tarsus, she would not be commanded.

One afternoon, while Antony was holding court in the marketplace, he began to notice the crowd whispering excitedly and hurrying toward the river.

Soon Antony was left alone with his guards. Everyone else had gone to gaze at Cleopatra. Plutarch tells us that "she came sailing up the river Cydnus in a barge with a poop of gold, its purple sails billowing in the wind, while her rowers caressed the water with oars of silver which dipped in time to the music of the flute, accompanied by pipes and lutes. Cleopatra herself reclined beneath a canopy of cloth of gold, dressed in the character of Venus...while on either side to complete the picture stood boys costumed as Cupids, who cooled her with fans." Splendid, indeed!

Cleopatra captivated Antony, just as she had Julius Caesar. This was to be the second—and last—love of her life.

Cleopatra's union with Mark Antony—as with Caesar before him—was no different from the marriages of other great rulers throughout history. It was as much a matter of politics as it was of love. Cleopatra had the wealth Antony needed to establish himself in the supreme position in Rome. In return, he could give her land and protect her from Roman invasion.

And yet, it seems obvious that they also felt love for each other, as the rest of their story shows.

Mark Antony was a handsome man, tall and muscular. He had such a noble face that he reminded people of the statues of Hercules. And though he was generous and brave, and loved by his soldiers, he did not have the intellect and steadiness of a man like Caesar. Antony was boisterous and enjoyed vulgar jokes. He was so fond of drinking that he was often associated with Bacchus, the god of wine. And he could be dangerously impulsive. It is not surprising that, enchanted by Cleopatra, he put aside his plans for war and followed her to Alexandria.

As well traveled as Antony was, he was surely impressed by this beautiful and sophisticated city with its grand avenues, temples, and gardens. Cleopatra's court was legendary for its luxury. It was said that the queen's cooks would roast as many as eight wild boars for one small dinner, putting one on the fire every half hour or so. Whenever the queen chose to dine, one of the boars would be perfectly done and ready to eat.

Her palace was grander than anything in Rome, richly decorated with marble, ebony, and gold. From its windows, Antony could gaze out over Alexandria's twin harbors, filled with more than a thousand ships from all over the world. Towering above the tall-masted ships stood the famous Pharos lighthouse, whose fire, magnified by mirrors, sent a beacon thirty-five miles out to sea. And beyond the harbor stretched the turquoise waters of the Mediterranean Sea, dazzling in the bright sunlight.

Antony found it hard to leave this place. He took to wearing Greek clothes and spent his days with Cleopatra, feasting, hunting, and playing games. Sometimes, late at night, they would put on servants' clothes and run about the streets knocking on people's doors and windows and laughing when the sleepy occupants cursed them.

There is a story in Plutarch's account about a fishing trip they took. Antony was catching nothing, so he secretly ordered a servant to swim under the boat and attach fish to his line. The queen soon discovered his game, and the following day she played a trick of her own. She, too, sent a servant under the boat with a fish for Antony to catch. To the delight of all, he brought up a dried and salted fish. After much laughter, she advised him affectionately to abandon fishing, as *his* sport was "to hunt cities and kingdoms and continents." Together, she and Antony could finish what she and Caesar had begun.

Over the next ten years, Antony and Cleopatra had three children. The oldest were twins, Alexander Helios and Cleopatra Selene, named after the Greek gods of the sun and the moon. The youngest was Ptolemy Philadelphus.

Antony made a political marriage with Octavian's sister, Octavia. And yet, he considered his marriage to Cleopatra to be the real one. For the rest of their lives, they would strive together for their great ambition, sharing the excitement, the danger, and the ultimate defeat.

In a lavish ceremony known as the Donations of Alexandria, Antony gave Cleopatra and her children a large part of Rome's eastern provinces, as well as some countries he hadn't conquered yet. Sitting on golden thrones, Antony was dressed as Dionysus (the Greek form of his favorite god, Bacchus) and Cleopatra as the Egyptian goddess Isis. Her four children, who sat below them on silver thrones, were dressed in the costumes of the different countries they were to rule. Caesarion had been his mother's co-ruler since the death of Ptolemy XIV, and now he received the title of King of Kings. And Cleopatra, as Queen of Kings, had realized her youthful dream of restoring Egypt to its former greatness.

Back in Rome, the people were shocked that Antony had given Roman land to a foreign ruler. Octavian began attacking him publicly and spreading tales that Antony was a weakling bewitched by the Queen of Egypt. He whipped up such hate and fear among the Roman people that everyone knew war was coming.

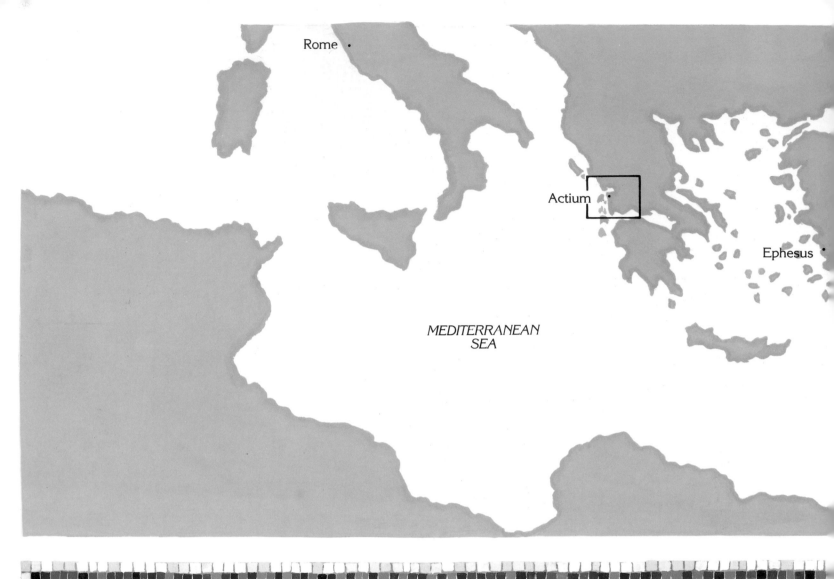

Rome

Actium

Ephesus

MEDITERRANEAN SEA

The fragile truce was finally broken when Antony divorced Octavia and sent a message that she and her children must leave his house in Rome. Octavian was outraged at this shabby treatment of his sister, an unusually sweet and virtuous woman, and he declared war. Cleverly, he did not declare it on Antony, a fellow Roman, but on Cleopatra, a foreign queen.

The forces of Antony and Cleopatra began to gather at Ephesus, on the coast of Asia Minor. They were joined by their Roman supporters, including almost a third of the senate. Friendly monarchs arrived from throughout the Near East, bringing troops and ships to fight with them. Not since Alexander had the military might of so many nations rested under one command.

The decisive battle took place off the coast of Greece. Octavian's army was camped on the north side of the Gulf of Ambracia. Antony and Cleopatra

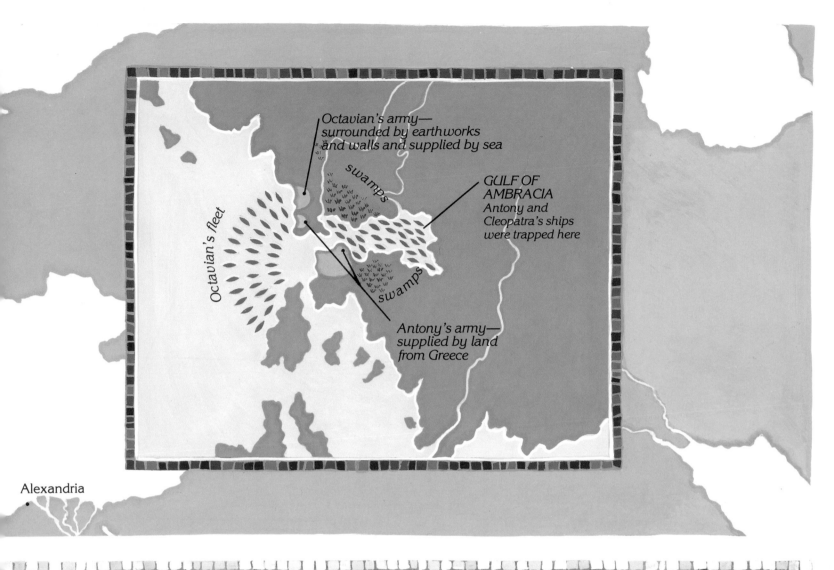

Octavian's army—
surrounded by earthworks
and walls and supplied by sea

swamps

GULF OF
AMBRACIA
Antony and
Cleopatra's ships
were trapped here

Octavian's fleet

swamps

Antony's army—
supplied by land
from Greece

Alexandria

were camped at Actium on the southern shore of the gulf, where their ships were anchored. Octavian's fleet, commanded by Marcus Agrippa, lay just outside the gulf, so that Antony's ships were trapped.

As the months passed, the men in Antony's camp became discouraged. Great numbers fell ill with malaria and dysentery, and so many rowing slaves were sick that much of the fleet could not be used. The officers resented Cleopatra so much that some of them deserted to Octavian.

Antony had to do *something*—either try to break the blockade of his ships or abandon them and retreat, hoping to win a land battle later on. Antony was more experienced in land warfare than he was on the sea. But Cleopatra wanted to save her fleet and argued strongly for a sea battle. Antony finally agreed.

He began preparing for battle. He ordered towers to be erected on the ships, fore and aft, from which his soldiers could fire arrows, rocks, and flaming objects at the enemy. Twenty thousand of his best soldiers came aboard.

Though a commander would not normally carry treasure into battle, Cleopatra's gold, silver, and jewels were brought aboard her ships, along with her baggage. Equally unusual, Antony ordered sails to be loaded on the ships. Sails, which were heavy, were used only for long voyages, not for a battle offshore, where the ships would be maneuvered by oars. This may be a clue to the great mystery of why the battle of Actium ended in such a surprising way.

Shortly after noon on September 2, 31 B.C., Antony's fleet lined up and rowed out of the harbor. In the rear were sixty of the best Egyptian ships, which Cleopatra commanded.

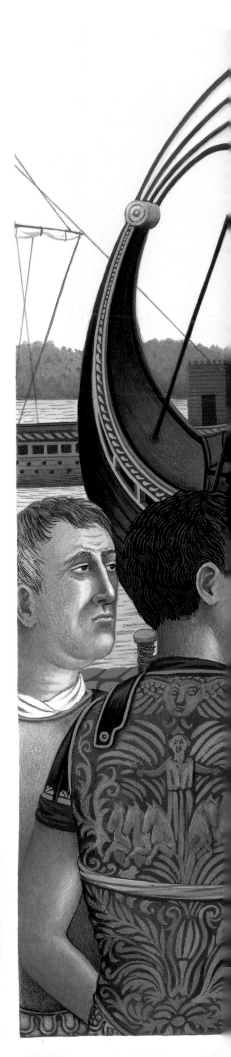

Once out of the channel, they fanned out to face Octavian's ships, and the battle of Actium began. Plutarch claims that long before it was clear who was going to win, Cleopatra's ships raised their sails and headed out into the open sea, toward Egypt.

Was she abandoning Antony and fleeing for her life? The Romans, who despised her, believed so. But the fact that her ships were equipped with sails and that her baggage and treasure were aboard suggests that this was planned. It is very likely that Cleopatra had agreed to go back to Egypt in order to appease Antony's officers, but only if she could save her fleet. She would need the ships to defend Alexandria.

But it is much more difficult to explain what happened next. For when Antony saw his wife sail away, he "abandoned and betrayed the men who were fighting and dying for his cause" and, taking a small, fast galley and two of his officers, hurried after her. Antony's fleet, overwhelmed and demoralized, surrendered to Octavian. The army soon did the same.

Antony's behavior is so astonishing for such a brave man that many historians believe there must be some hidden explanation. Most likely the pair had always intended to retreat and save the treasure and as many ships as possible. Later, Octavian's propaganda made Cleopatra seem a traitor and Antony a coward. But we will never know for sure what really happened, or why.

The great empire Cleopatra had so recently acquired was gone. Even Egypt would not be hers for long, for Octavian was sure to come after them and take that, too. Although Cleopatra knew she had no hope of keeping her throne, perhaps Caesarion, now seventeen, might be permitted to rule. Three times she wrote to Octavian, pleading her son's case. Octavian did not reply.

If that didn't work, she had another idea. She would escape with her army, her ships, and her vast treasure to some friendly Asian land, there to rebuild her strength and perhaps, someday, win back her empire. She ordered her ships to be lifted out of the sea and hauled on rollers over several miles of desert from the Mediterranean Sea to the Red Sea. There they would be safe from Octavian and be in a position to escape. But this bold plan was abandoned before the whole fleet could be moved, for the Arabians of Nabataea, hoping to win Octavian's favor, set the ships afire.

Antony did not have Cleopatra's amazing powers of recuperation. While she was trying to find a way out of their awful situation, he fell into a state of depression and despair. He even went so far as to have a little hut built for himself, and for a time he lived there alone, sunk in bitterness and self-pity.

As Octavian's armies converged on Egypt from the east and the west, Cleopatra began making more desperate plans. She had prepared a grand tomb for herself, next to that of Alexander the Great. She gathered her gold, silver, and jewels and hid them inside. Then she began investigating various poisons, seeking one that would act quickly and painlessly. Plutarch claims that she had them tested on prisoners condemned to death. Finding that "the drugs which acted most quickly caused the victim to die in agony, while the milder poisons were slow to take effect, she went on to examine…various venomous creatures." She concluded that nothing would assure her a swift and painless death like the bite of the asp, a poisonous snake.

With Octavian's army just outside the city, Antony pulled himself together and prepared to defend Alexandria. There is a legend that the night before the battle, the sounds of singing and dancing were heard in the darkened streets, as if a parade of revelers were passing by on its way out the eastern gate. People said it was the god Bacchus, deserting Antony.

The following day, what remained of the Egyptian fleet took the god's example and defected to Octavian. The army was quickly defeated, and Antony fled back to the palace.

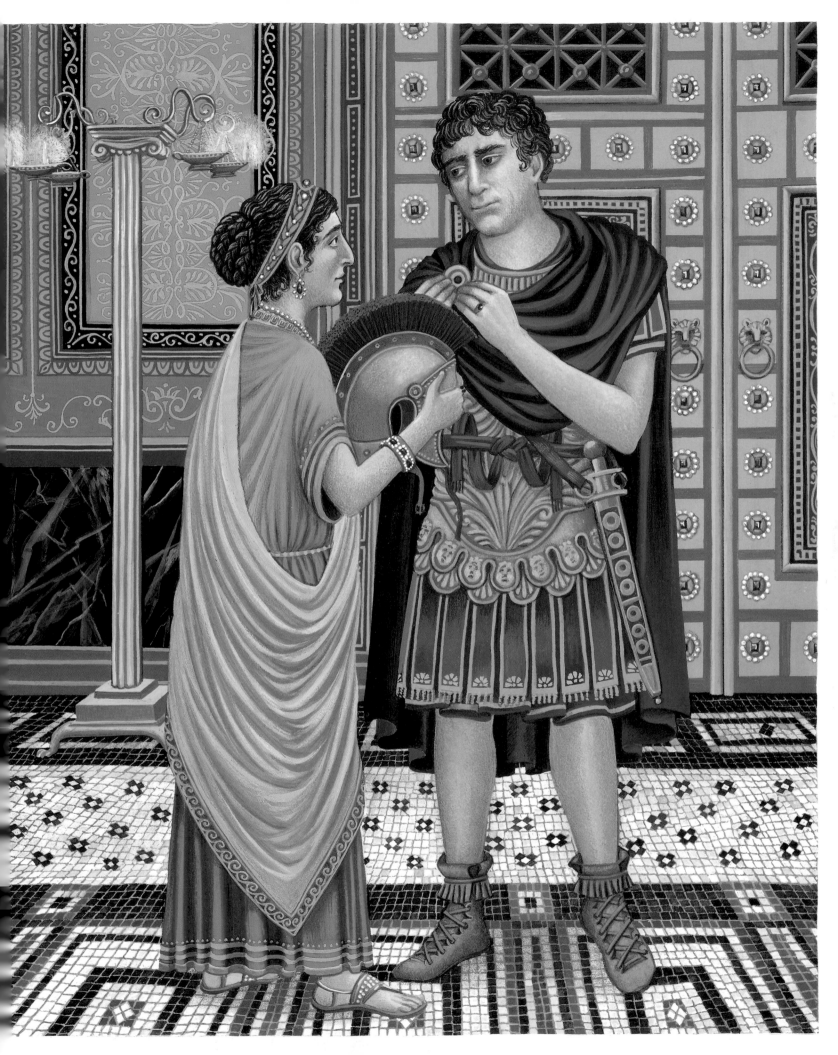

When Antony returned, he could not find Cleopatra. Already frantic and distraught, he then got word that she was dead. With nothing left to live for, he threw himself on his sword. Poor Antony was not even successful at this. Though wounded and in pain, he still lived. As he lay suffering, a messenger came to him bearing the heartbreaking truth: The first message had been false. Cleopatra was alive, barricaded in her tomb, and she begged him to come to her.

Two slaves carried the bleeding Antony to Cleopatra's tomb. Since the doors were sealed, the queen let down ropes from a window on the second floor. With much difficulty, she and her servants brought him inside and carried him to a bed. Cleopatra was beside herself with grief. Plutarch says that even as he was dying, Antony tried to comfort her. He begged her not to pity him, for he had achieved glory and fame. His was an honorable death, conquered as he was by a fellow Roman.

And so Antony found peace in death, but Cleopatra's trials were not quite over. Some time later, one of Octavian's men came to the door to speak with the queen, trying to persuade her to come out. While she was distracted by this conversation, Octavian's men brought a ladder around to the very window through which Antony had been carried. Once inside, they rushed down the stairs and took her captive.

Octavian allowed Cleopatra to give Antony a lavish funeral, as befitted a king. Then he ordered her to make ready for a voyage to Rome. She knew what would happen to her there. Cleopatra would be the highlight of Octavian's triumphal parade. She would be led in chains through the streets of Rome, where the crowd would mock and curse her.

Before she was to leave, Octavian allowed her to visit Antony's tomb one last time. Plutarch says she wept bitterly and begged the gods to save her from the terrible shame that faced her. She wished only to join Antony in death.

Then, laying a garland of flowers on his grave, she returned to her rooms.
There she bathed and dressed with care and, reclining on her golden couch,
enjoyed a sumptuous meal. It was to be her last.

A peasant arrived with a basket of figs for the queen. The guards com-
mented agreeably on how large and fine the figs were. The man laughed and
offered them some, but they declined, so he took them in to Cleopatra.

Her meal finished, the queen sent a sealed letter to Octavian, then
dismissed everyone except her two most trusted servants.

When Octavian read the letter, he was alarmed. In it Cleopatra asked that she be buried in the same tomb as Antony. Certain that she intended to take her own life, Octavian sent officers hurrying to her room. There they found her, beautifully laid out in her royal robes. She was already dead. One of her women lay dying at her feet, and the other, with what remained of her strength, was adjusting the queen's crown.

That is the story as Plutarch tells it. No one knows exactly how she died, except that she must have taken poison in some form. Many believe that she had arranged for a poisonous asp to be smuggled in, hidden among the figs.

Cleopatra was only thirty-nine when she died, in the year 30 B.C. She was buried with Antony, as she had wished. Of the many successors of Alexander the Great, only she became a legend as Alexander had. She had ruled Egypt for twenty-one years and, having raised her country to new heights, had brought about its downfall. In a world where women had little power, she had fought to control the destiny of nations. And if she had succeeded in her great venture, it would have been Cleopatra and her descendants who ruled the Western world, instead of the emperors of Rome.

EPILOGUE

Egypt became a part of the Roman Empire. Octavian, under the new name of Augustus Caesar, became the first Emperor of Rome, bringing the republic to an end. He ruled with wisdom and prudence and lived to be an old man. After his death, the Romans made him a god. It was rumored that he was poisoned by his wife.

Caesarion, who had been sent to India for safety by his mother, never got there. He was betrayed by his tutor and fell into Octavian's hands. Octavian had been advised that "it is bad to have too many Caesars," and so he ordered the young man put to death.

Cleopatra Selene was made to walk in Octavian's triumph, then lived in Rome with the amazingly generous Octavia. When Selene grew up, she was married to King Juba II of Numidia, a great scholar and historian. Juba wrote a history of Rome, which has since been lost but was probably one of the sources Plutarch used to write about Cleopatra.

The fate of Alexander Helios and little Ptolemy Philadelphus is not clear, though they too probably were displayed in Octavian's triumph. Most sources claim their lives were spared because of their youth.

No one knows what became of the tombs of Antony, Cleopatra, or Alexander the Great. The Pharos lighthouse stood for over a thousand more years and survived two earthquakes before crumbling into the sea. Of ancient Alexandria, almost nothing remains.

PRONUNCIATION GUIDE

Alexander Helios   AL-ex-AND-er HEE-lee-ose
Ambracia   Am-BRAY-sha
Apollodorus   Uh-PALL-uh-DORE-us
Bacchus   BAH-kus
Caesar   SEE-zer
Caesarion   See-ZARE-ee-un
Cilicia   Sih-LISH-uh
Cleopatra Selene   KLEE-uh-PAT-ruh Suh-LEE-nee
Cydnus   SID-nus
Dionysus   Di-uh-NY-sis
Ephesus   EF-ih-sus
Euclid   YOO-klid
Isis   EYE-sis
Marcus Aemilius Lepidus   MAR-kus Ay-MEE-lee-us LEH-puh-dus
Nabataea   NAH-buh-TEE-uh
Pharaohs   FAY-rows
Pharos   FAH-ros
Plutarch   PLOO-tark
Ptolemy   TALL-uh-mee
Ptolemy Philadelphus   TALL-uh-mee Fill-uh-DELL-fuss
Thutmose   Thoot-MO-suh

BIBLIOGRAPHY

The Brooklyn Museum. *Cleopatra's Egypt: Age of the Ptolemies*. 1988. Exhibition catalog.

Brown, Blanche R. *Ptolemaic Paintings and Mosaics and The Alexandrian Style*. Cambridge, Massachusetts: Archaeological Institute of America, 1957.

Grant, Michael. *Cleopatra*. New York: Simon and Schuster, 1972.

Hughes-Hallett, Lucy. *Cleopatra: Histories, Dreams and Distortions*. New York: HarperCollins, 1990.

Huzar, Eleanor Goltz. *Mark Antony: A Biography*. Minneapolis: University of Minnesota Press, 1978.

Plutarch. *Fall of the Roman Republic: Six Lives by Plutarch*. Translated by Rex Warner. New York: Penguin Books, 1980.

Plutarch. *Makers of Rome: Nine Lives by Plutarch*. Translated by Ian Scott-Kilvert. New York: Penguin Books, 1978.

Suetonius Tranquillus, Caius. *The Lives of the Twelve Caesars*. New York: The Book League of America, 1937.

Volkmann, Hans. *Cleopatra: A Study in Politics and Propaganda*. Translated by T. J. Cadoux. New York: Sagamore Press, 1958.

Recommended for younger readers:
Asimov, Isaac. *The Egyptians*. Boston: Houghton Mifflin Company, 1967.

Hoobler, Dorothy and Thomas. *Cleopatra*. New York: Chelsea House Publishers, 1986.